Japanese
DECORATIVE DESIGNS
COLORING BOOK

The decorative designs featured here are timeless examples of Japanese artistry. Although little is known of their creators or the actual dates of their creation, such designs reflect Japanese artists' historically deep appreciation of beauty in art and nature and have influenced tastes in everything from textiles to paper goods, furniture to fine art. Europe and North America have long been enamored of Japanese design and aesthetics, particularly since Japan opened its political and economic borders in 1868, providing the impetus for an unprecedented exchange of arts and culture with the West.

The twenty-two textile designs selected for this coloring book reside in the collections of the Fine Arts Museums of San Francisco, which include more than 13,000 textiles and costumes from traditions around the world.

We've left the last page of this book blank in case you might be inspired to draw and color your own decorative design.

**Fine Arts
Museums of
San Francisco**

Pomegranate

Included here are adaptations of Japanese textile designs by anonymous Japanese artists. The original designs are in the collection of the Achenbach Foundation for Graphic Arts, at the Fine Arts Museums of San Francisco.

© 2018 Fine Arts Museums of San Francisco
www.famsf.org
Line drawings © Pomegranate Communications, Inc.

Item No. CB195

Designed by Patrice Morris

PRINTED IN KOREA

Pomegranate Communications, Inc.
19018 NE Portal Way, Portland OR 97230
800 227 1428   www.pomegranate.com

Distributed by Pomegranate Europe Ltd.
'number three', Siskin Drive, Middlemarch Business Park
Coventry CV3 4FJ, UK
+44 (0)24 7621 4461   sales@pomegranate.com

Pomegranate's mission is to invigorate, illuminate, and inspire through art.

This product is in compliance with the CPSIA. A General Conformity Certificate and tracking information are available through Pomegranate.

27 26 25 24 23 22 21 20 19 18   10 9 8 7 6 5 4 3 2 1

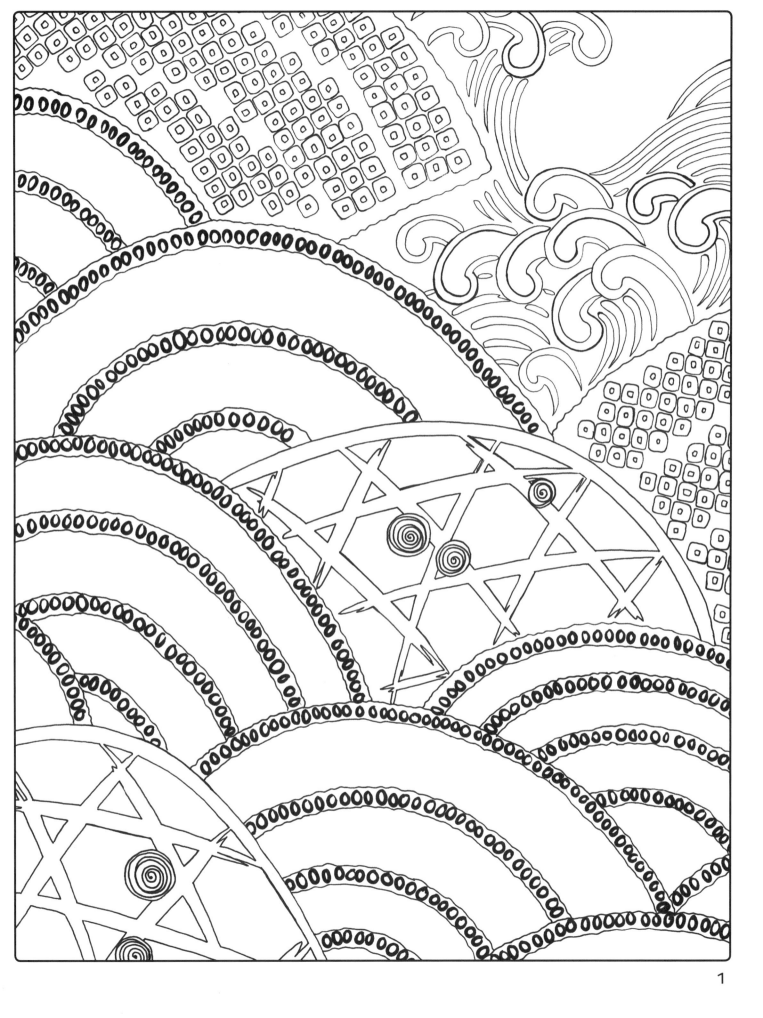

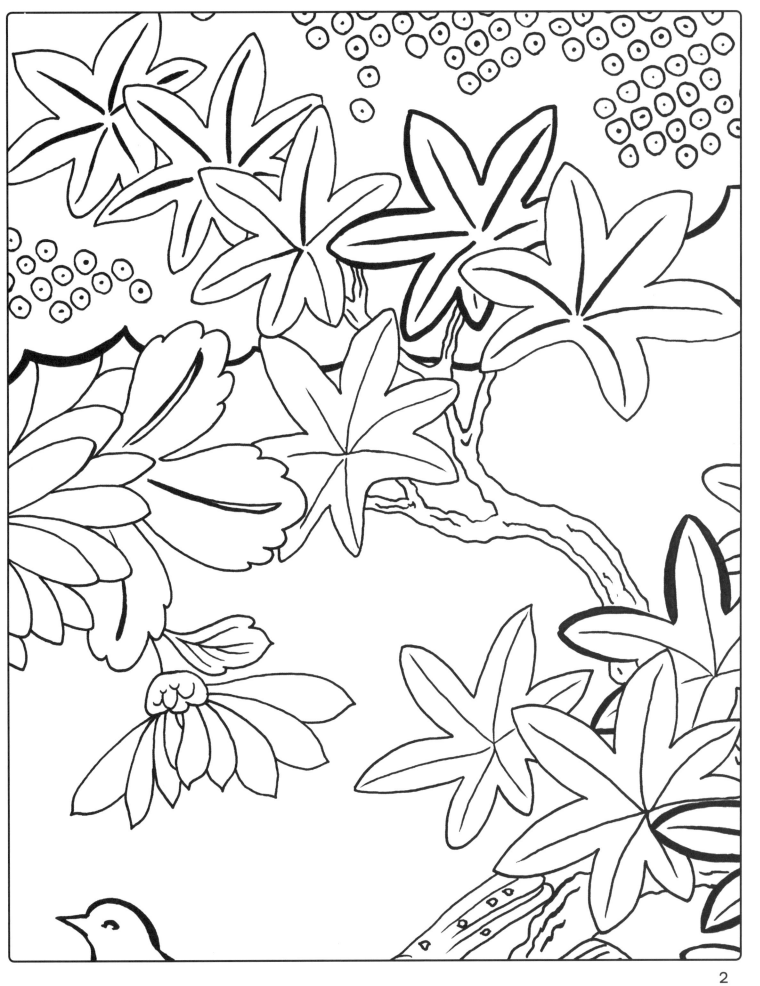

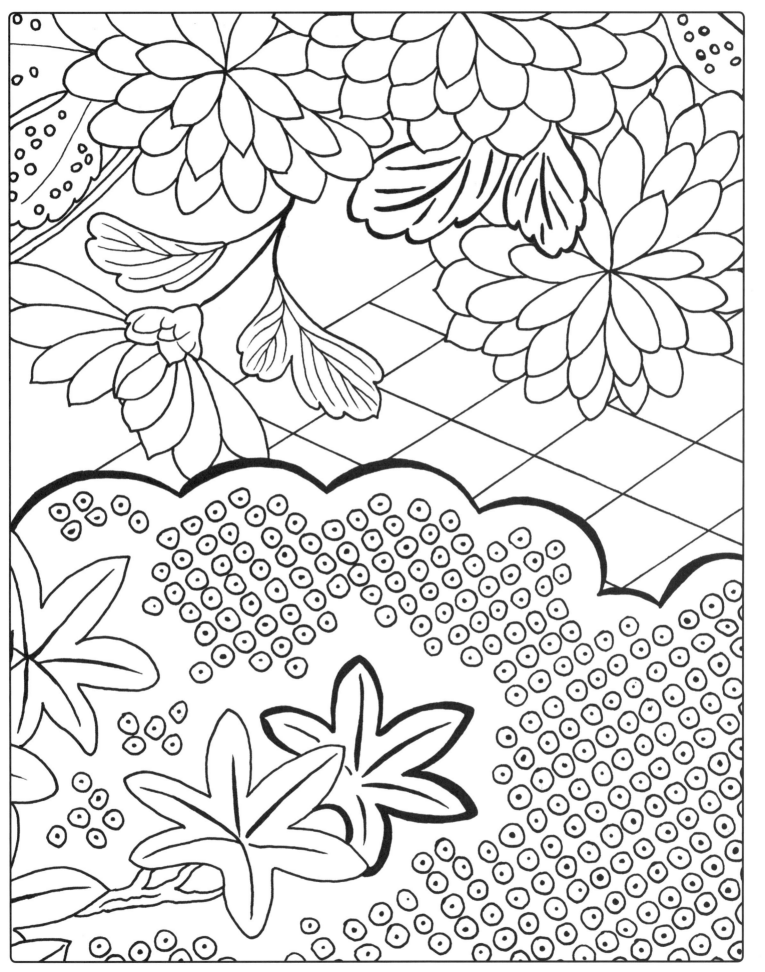

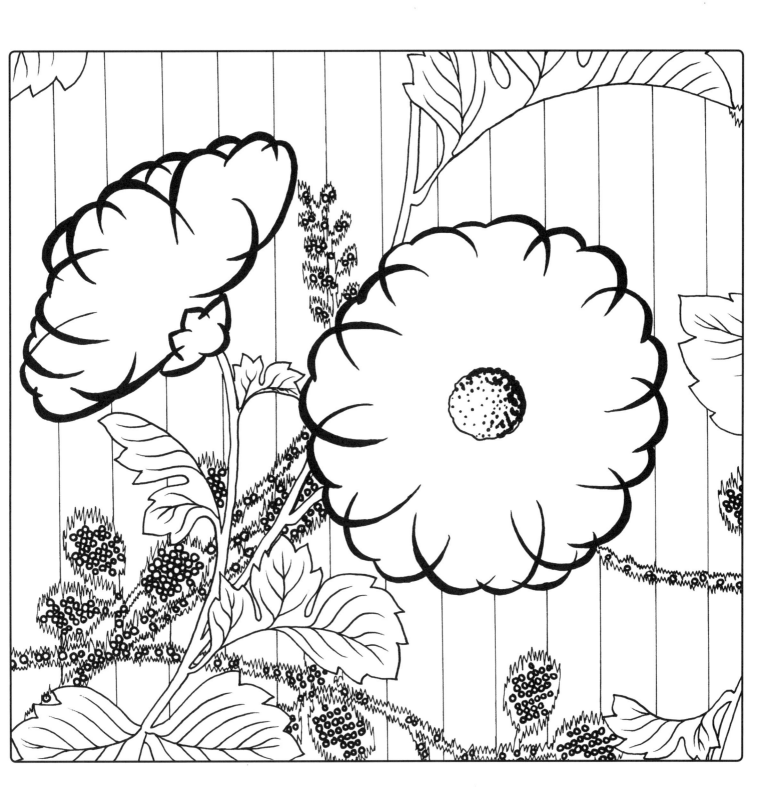

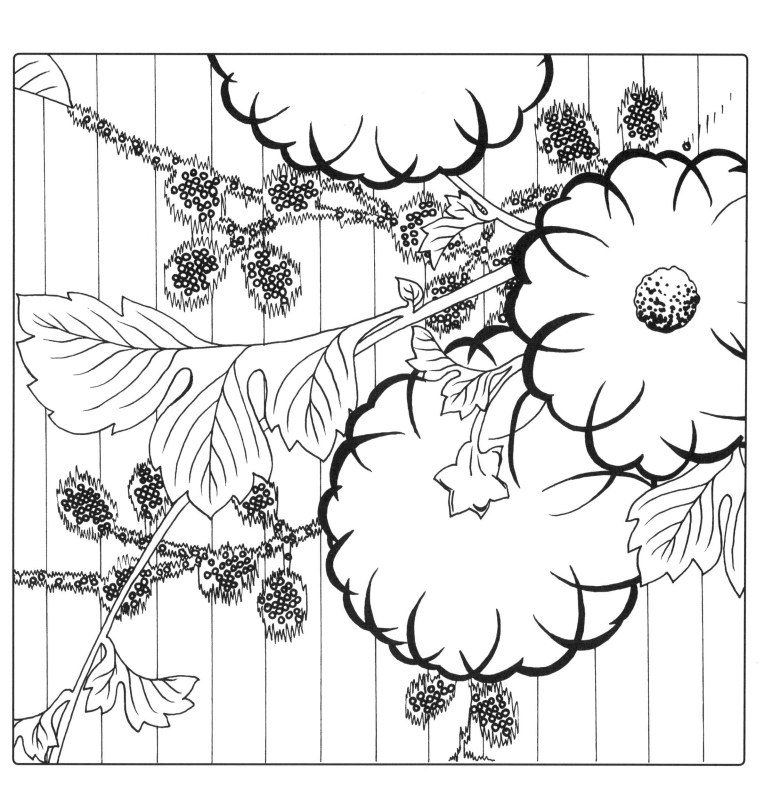

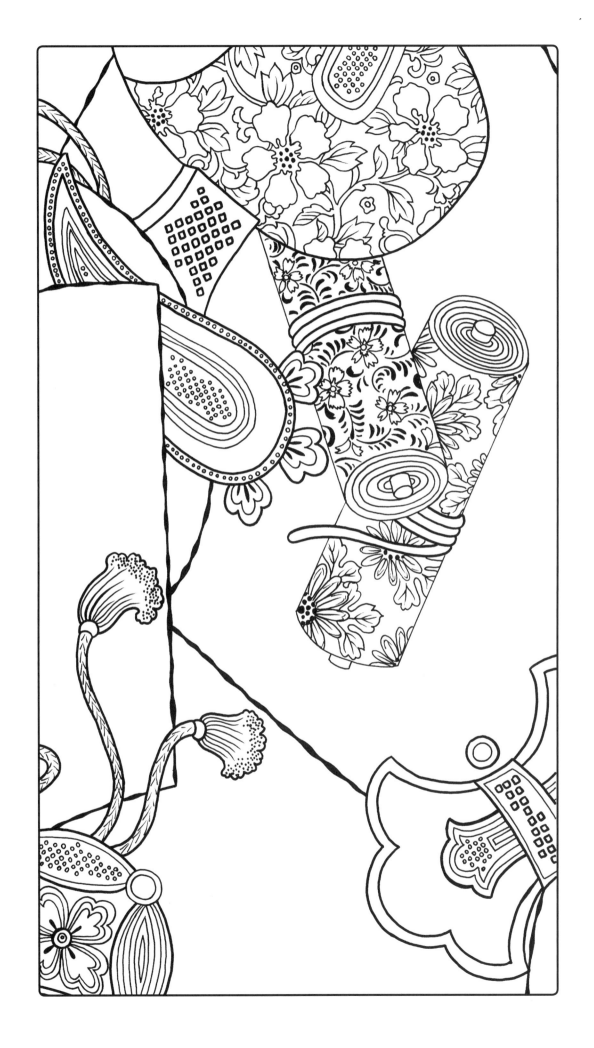

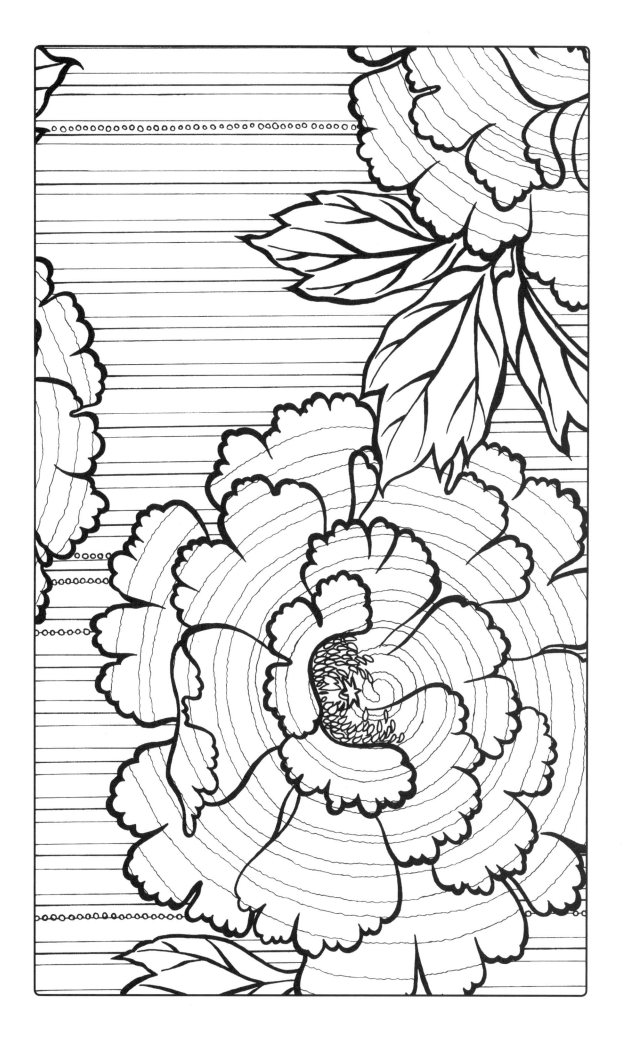

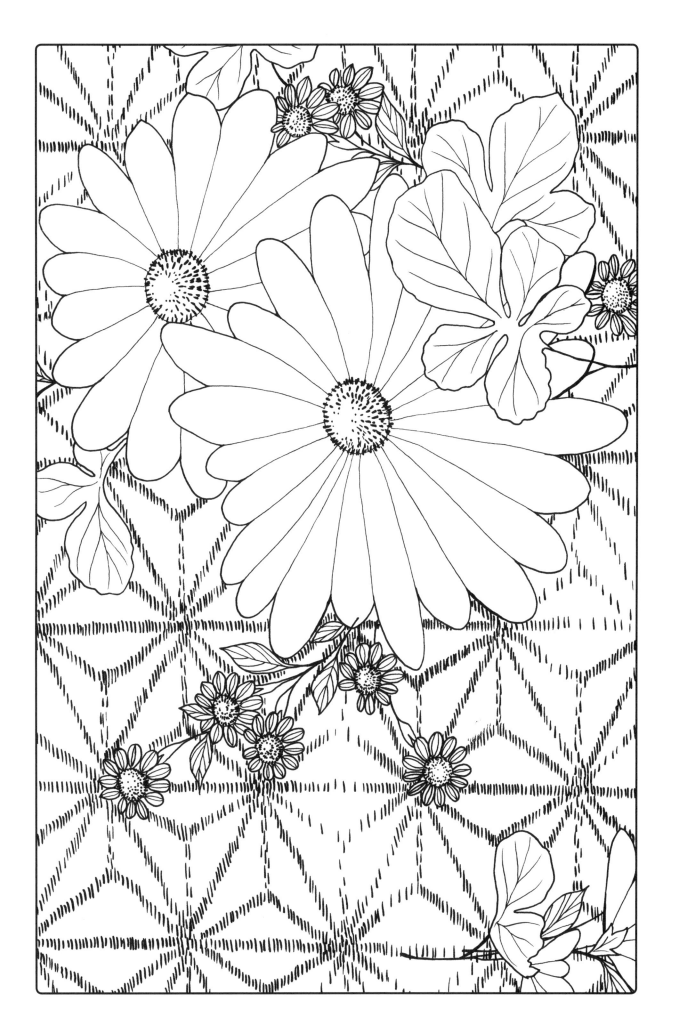

8

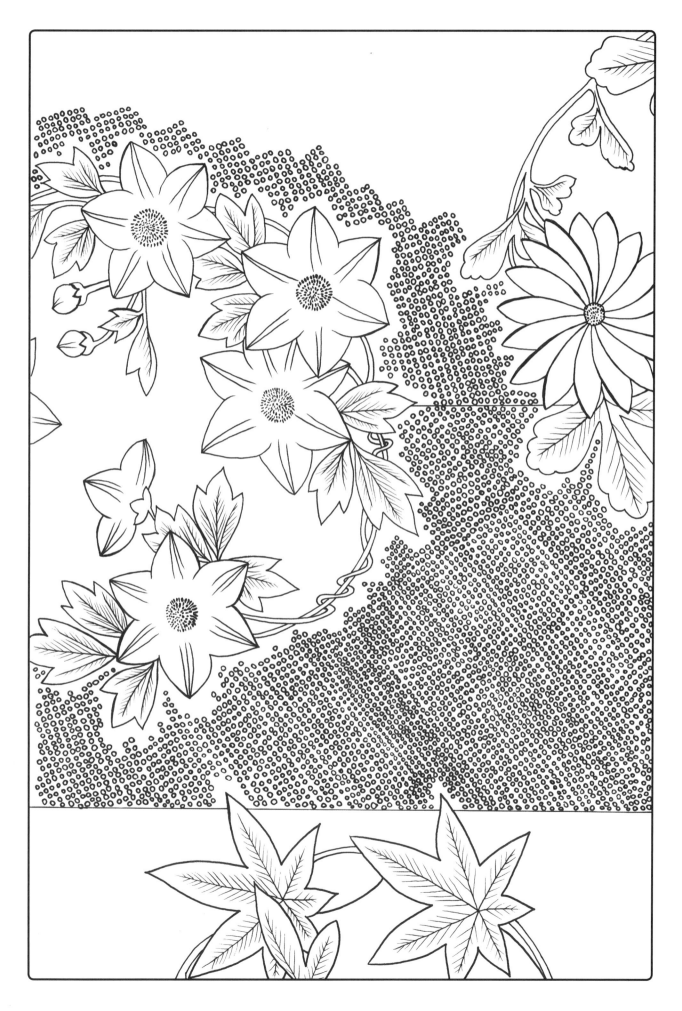

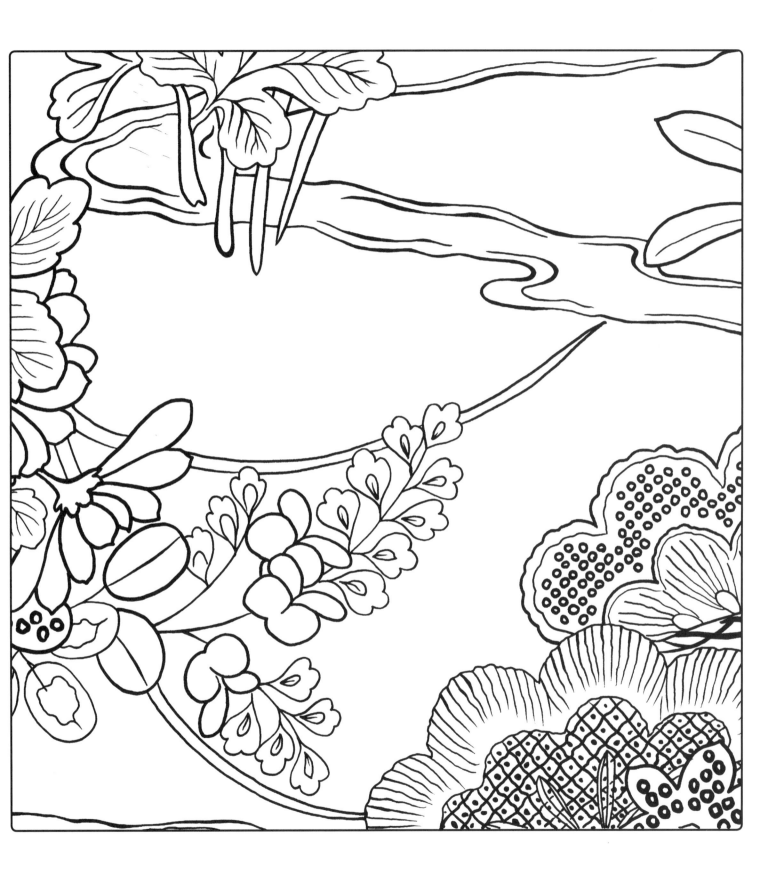

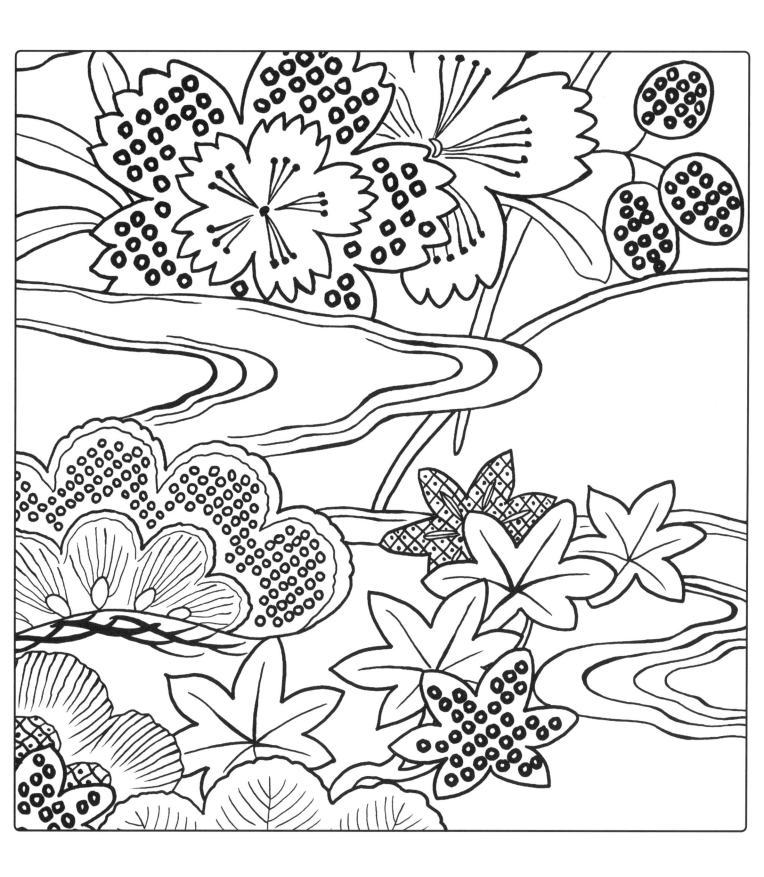

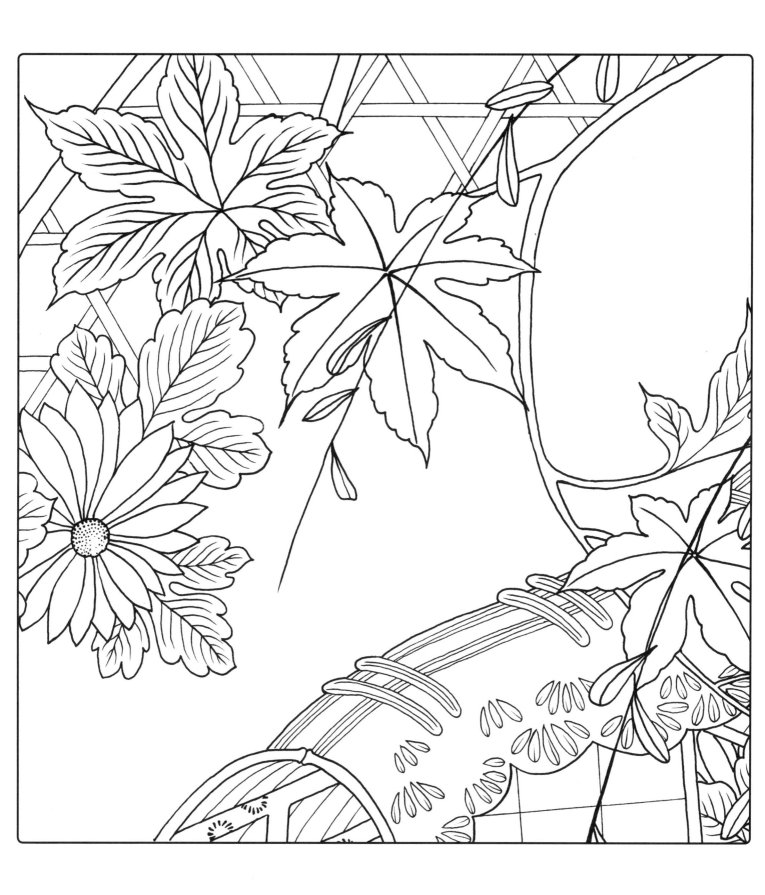

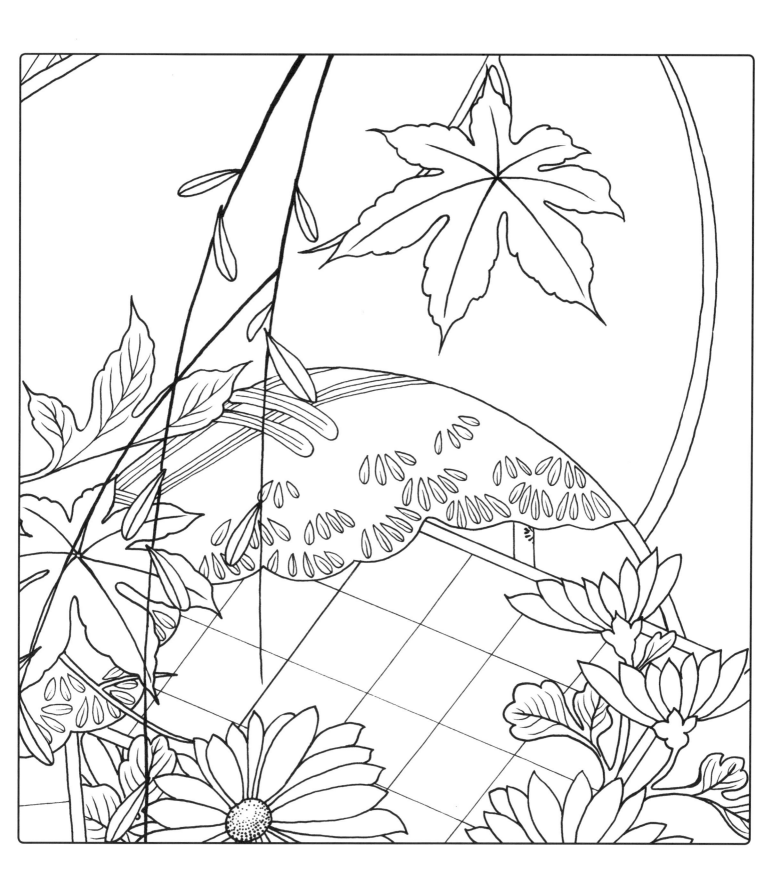

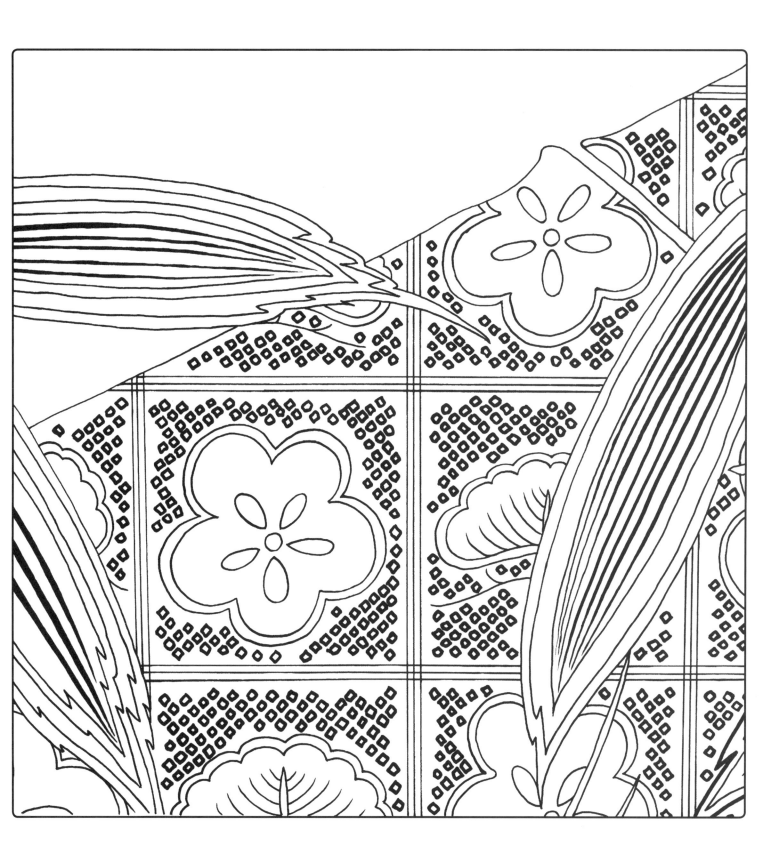

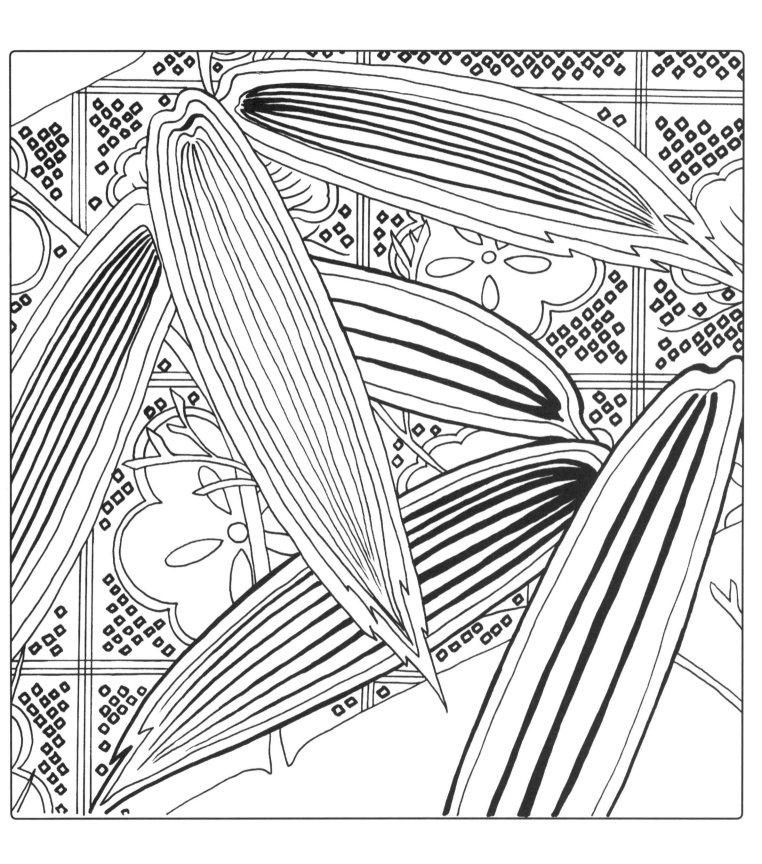

15

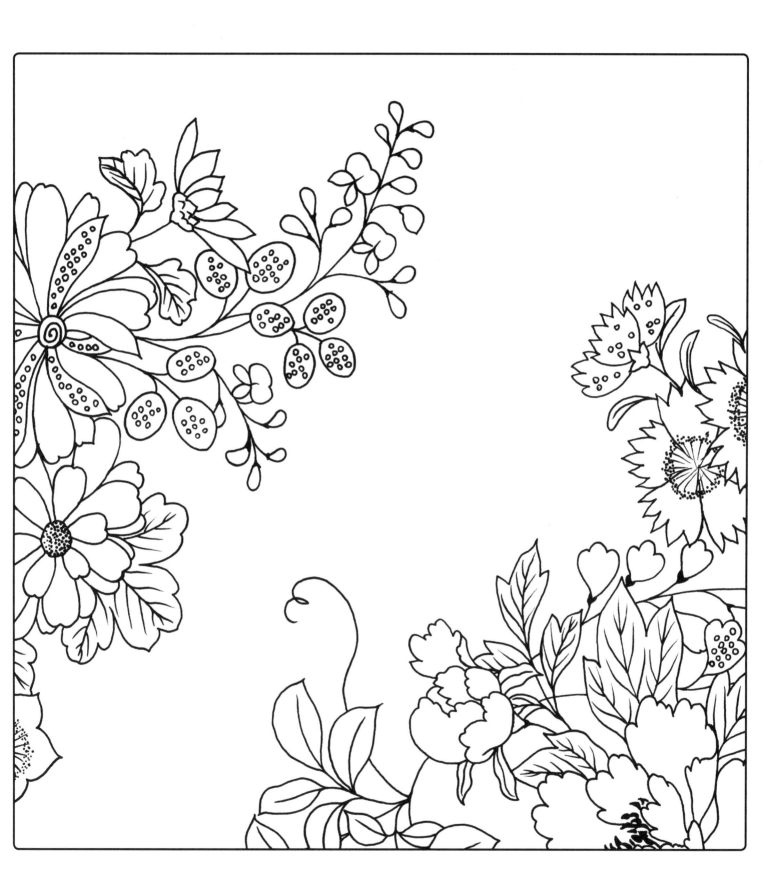

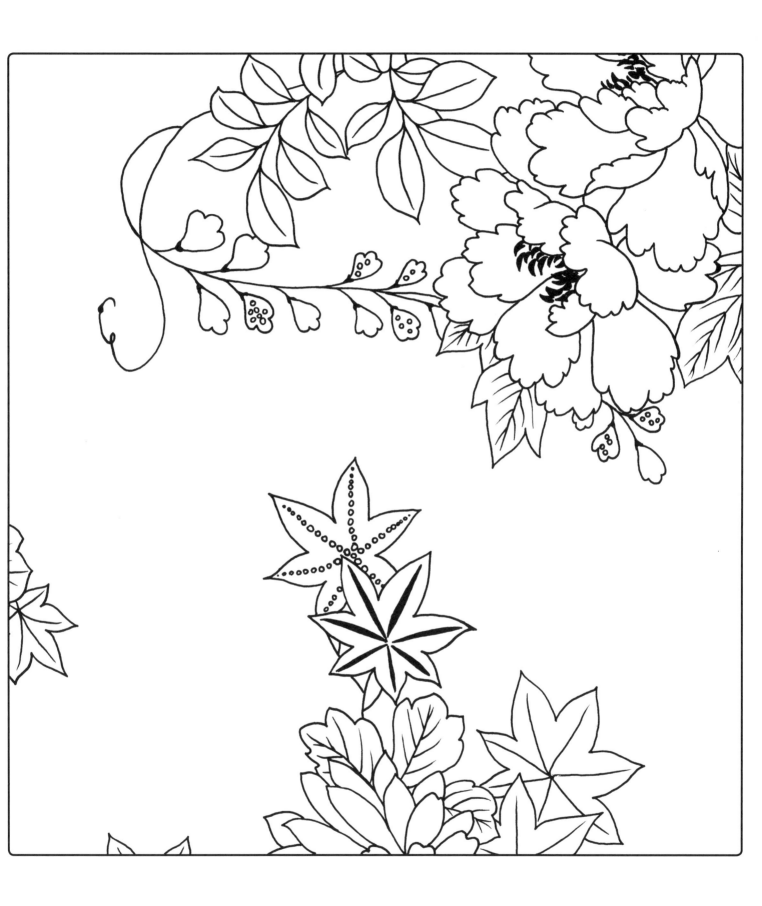

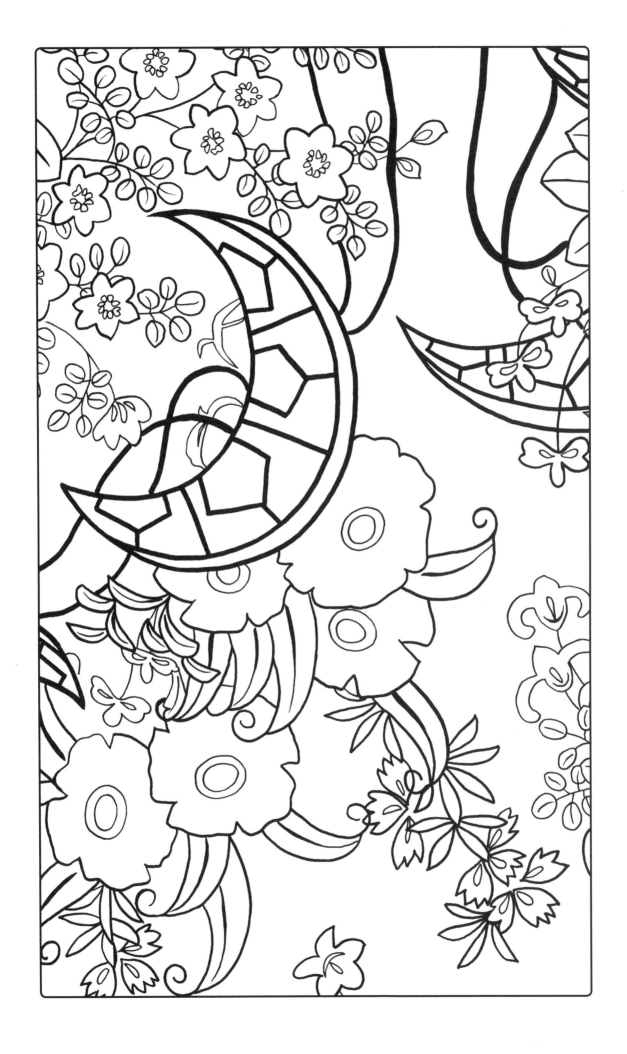

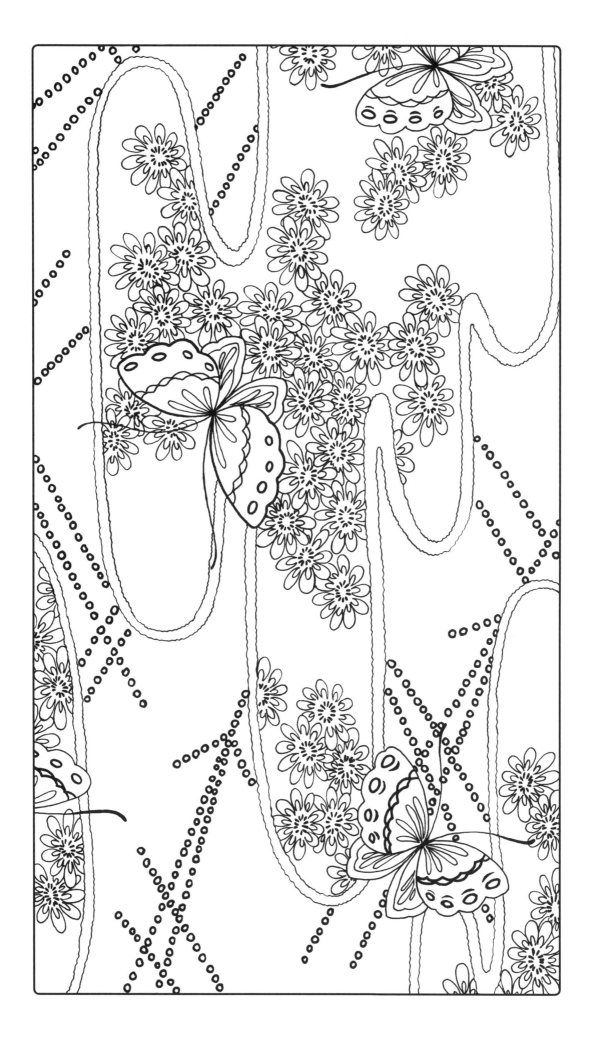

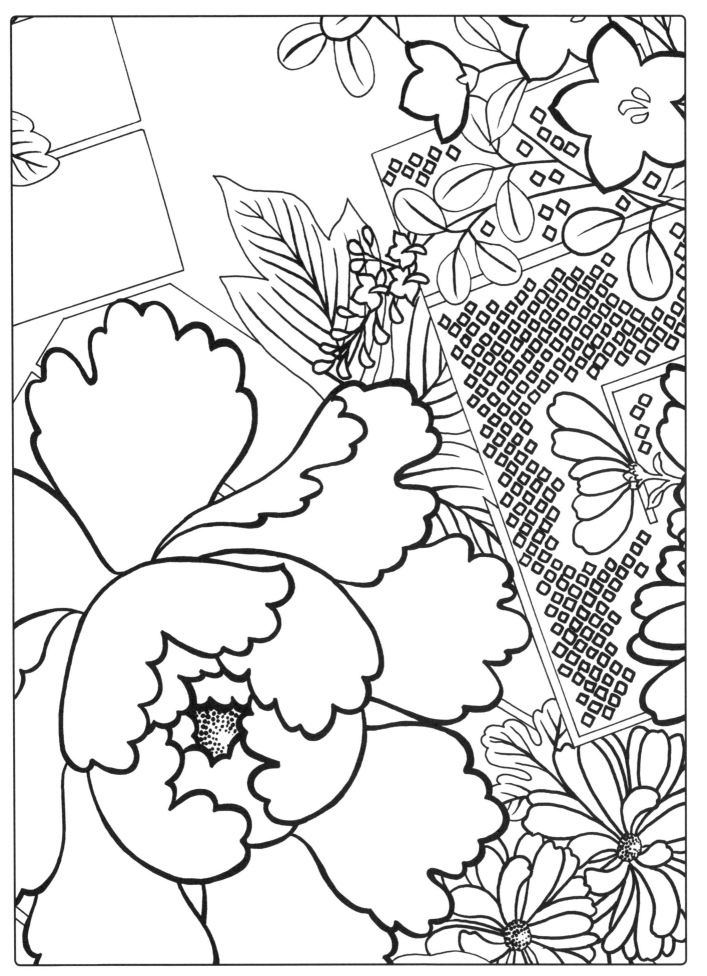

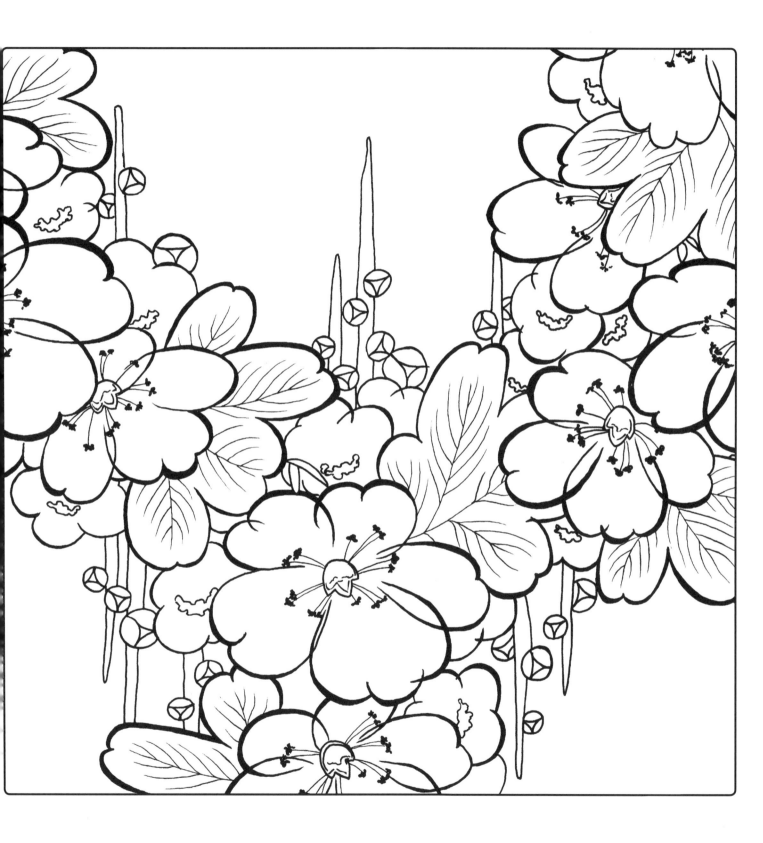

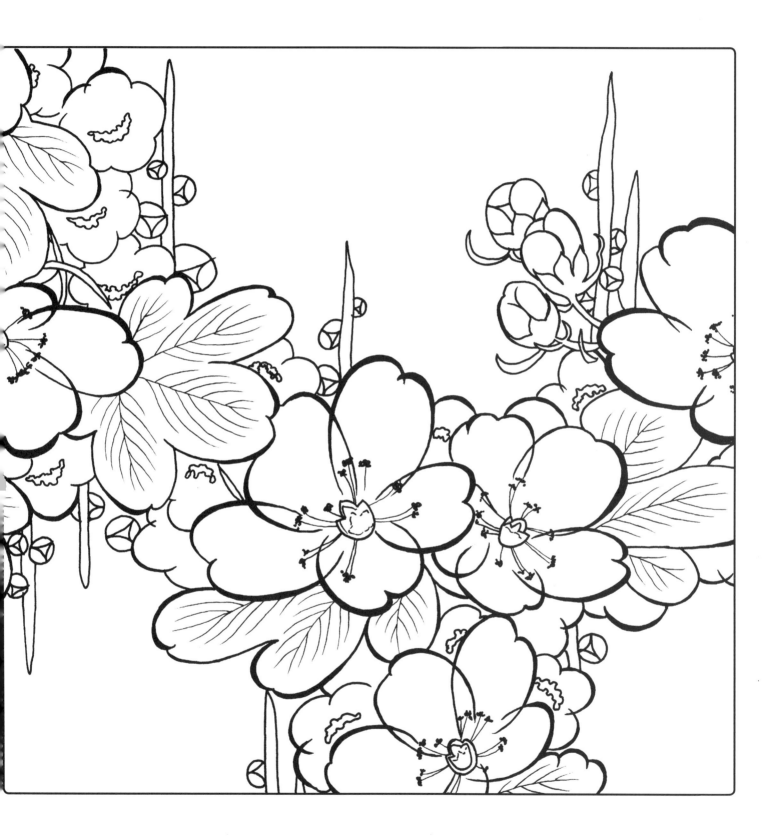

Draw and color your own picture here!